Christmas Magic

Anxiety & Stress Relief Coloring Book

For Adults

Patricia Mary O'Brien

The Preview

Thank You for your purchase...

...Bring our book to life with color...

As a thank you gift, we will send you 25 of our best
Adult Coloring Pages for "Free" to print and color.
Just send us an email with the subject line,
25 Adult Coloring Pages to:
obriensgoods@hotmail.com

We appreciate your considerate and honest reviews
to let us know how we are doing...

Sincerely,
Patricia Mary O'Brien

Ink saturation page for Gel Pen and Marker coloring

Ink saturation page for Gel Pen and Marker coloring

Ink saturation page for Gel Pen and Marker coloring

Ink saturation page for Gel Pen and Marker coloring

Peace

Ink saturation page for Gel Pen and Marker coloring

Ink saturation page for Gel Pen and Marker coloring

Ink saturation page for Gel Pen and Marker coloring

Ink saturation page for Gel Pen and Marker coloring

Ink saturation page for Gel Pen and Marker coloring

Ink saturation page for Gel Pen and Marker coloring

Ink saturation page for Gel Pen and Marker coloring

Ink saturation page for Gel Pen and Marker coloring

Ink saturation page for Gel Pen and Marker coloring

Ink saturation page for Gel Pen and Marker coloring

Ink saturation page for Gel Pen and Marker coloring

Happy
Christmas

Ink saturation page for Gel Pen and Marker coloring

Ink saturation page for Gel Pen and Marker coloring

Ink saturation page for Gel Pen and Marker coloring

Ink saturation page for Gel Pen and Marker coloring

Ink saturation page for Gel Pen and Marker coloring

Ink saturation page for Gel Pen and Marker coloring

Ink saturation page for Gel Pen and Marker coloring

Ink saturation page for Gel Pen and Marker coloring

Ink saturation page for Gel Pen and Marker coloring

Ink saturation page for Gel Pen and Marker coloring

Ink saturation page for Gel Pen and Marker coloring

Ink saturation page for Gel Pen and Marker coloring

Ink saturation page for Gel Pen and Marker coloring

Ink saturation page for Gel Pen and Marker coloring

Happy
Holidays

Ink saturation page for Gel Pen and Marker coloring

Ink saturation page for Gel Pen and Marker coloring

Ink saturation page for Gel Pen and Marker coloring

Merry
Christmas

Ink saturation page for Gel Pen and Marker coloring

Ink saturation page for Gel Pen and Marker coloring

Ink saturation page for Gel Pen and Marker coloring

Merry
Christmas

Ink saturation page for Gel Pen and Marker coloring

Ink saturation page for Gel Pen and Marker coloring

Ink saturation page for Gel Pen and Marker coloring

HAPPY CHRISTMAS!

Ink saturation page for Gel Pen and Marker coloring

Ink saturation page for Gel Pen and Marker coloring

Ink saturation page for Gel Pen and Marker coloring

Ink saturation page for Gel Pen and Marker coloring

Ink saturation page for Gel Pen and Marker coloring

Ink saturation page for Gel Pen and Marker coloring

SANTA
CRUZ

Ink saturation page for Gel Pen and Marker coloring

Ink saturation page for Gel Pen and Marker coloring

Ink saturation page for Gel Pen and Marker coloring

Ink saturation page for Gel Pen and Marker coloring

Ink saturation page for Gel Pen and Marker coloring

Ink saturation page for Gel Pen and Marker coloring

Ink saturation page for Gel Pen and Marker coloring

Ink saturation page for Gel Pen and Marker coloring

Ink saturation page for Gel Pen and Marker coloring

Ink saturation page for Gel Pen and Marker coloring

Ink saturation page for Gel Pen and Marker coloring

Ink saturation page for Gel Pen and Marker coloring

Ink saturation page for Gel Pen and Marker coloring

Ink saturation page for Gel Pen and Marker coloring

About the Author

Patricia Mary O'Brien is the author of "Mr. Calou Owns the Zoo", "Giggly Piggly Goes to The City", and over 75 publications that include children's educational, coloring, and activity books.
An artist, a musician, and a painter, she enjoys being creative leading her to write and illustrate books.

Publications

- Mr. Calou Owns the Zoo
- Giggly Piggly Goes to The City
- Pretty Princess Coloring Book-Princesses and Castles
- Be Yourself Girls Coloring Book-Building Confidence
- Sight Words Workbook-Sight Words Activities for Reading, Tracing, Writing and Spelling
- Preschool Plus Coloring Book-Airplanes and More
- Tracing Numbers 1-20 and Spelling
- Fashion and Flare Coloring Book-Easy and Detailed Graphics
- Easter Coloring Book - Let's Go on an Easter Egg Hunt
- Be My Valentine Coloring Book-Adorable Valentine Animals
- Scissor Skills Activity Book-Learning to Use Scissors
- Learn To Print Tracing Book-Letters, Words, Numbers, Shapes, and Coloring
- Learn to Draw Animals
- Scissor Skills Activity Book-Christmas
- I'm Learning to Write-Cursive Handwriting for Children
- Christmas Coloring Book
- Huge Activity Book-Over 200 Pages for Hours of Learning
- Sight Words Activity Book
- Tracing Numbers 1-20 Activity Book
- Preschool Plus Coloring Book
- The Little Book of Gnomes Coloring Book
- Preschool Rainy-Day Coloring and Activities
- Dot To Dot 100 Pictures - Learn to Count-Draw-Color
- Adult Coloring Book 1, 2, 3, 4, 5, 6, 7 and 8
- Adult Coloring Book 9 - Halloween
- Adult Coloring Book 10 - Christmas
- Adult Coloring Book 11 - Doodle Art
- Adult Coloring Book 12 - The Special Garden
- Adult Coloring Book 13 - ZEN ART
- Adult Coloring Book 14 - Animals
- Adult Coloring Book 15 - Flowers & Scenery